AF415528

THE JUNGLE ISN'T OUT THERE

a path to meditation

STEVE PRICE

Copyright ©2020 by Steve Price
All rights reserved
Printed in the United States
ISBN 9798688507829

THIS BOOK IS NOT INTENDED TO TREAT OR CURE ANY MENTAL, PHYSICAL OR EMOTIONAL CONDITION. MEDITATION MAY CAUSE BOREDOM, IRRITATION, ANGER, SADNESS, RESTLESSNESS, DROWSINESS, NAUSEA, CONFUSION, CLARITY, TINGLING, DISCOMFORT, LAUGHTER, INSIGHT, OUT-OF-BODY EXPERIENCES, ELATION, MISERY, TRANQUILITY, OR ENLIGHTENMENT. CONSULT WITH YOUR DOCTOR OR THERAPIST BEFORE STARTING A MEDITATION PRACTICE. PRACTICING UNDER THE GUIDANCE OF A QUALIFIED INSTRUCTOR IS RECOMMENDED. MEDITATION MAY BE CONTRAINDICATED FOR CERTAIN INDIVIDUALS. IF YOU FEEL YOU MAY HARM YOURSELF OR OTHERS, SEEK PROFESSIONAL HELP IMMEDIATELY.

THE JUNGLE

You know the saying, *It's a jungle out there*?

Well, the jungle isn't out there. It's in here, in our mind.

This book is a map of that inner jungle, and how to make it your kingdom.

The approach is nothing new. In fact, it's thousands of years old. It was developed by a sage named Patanjali, sometimes referred to as the Jungle Doctor. He specialized In dispelling the poisons of the human mind.

What the Jungle Doctor prescribes is a potent combination of wisdom, understanding and meditation.

Whether you take this medicine is entirely up to you.

You can be the lion or you can be the monkey.

It's your jungle.

A father and son pull up to a restaurant. The boy sees a homeless man talking to himself.

"Dad, look at that guy. He's crazy."

"He's no different than we are," the father replies. "It's just that he's talking out loud, and we're doing it in our heads."

This is monkey mind, the constant chatter that distracts, exhausts, confuses, and isolates us.

What to do?

The Jungle Doctor has a step-by-step procedure. It starts with examining the causes.

"Who the hell do you think you are?"

Whenever my father asked me this, I was stumped. It had less to do with the vein bulging in his forehead and more with the fact that I had no clue who I was.

At that moment, I was a kid being yelled at for talking back. A wise-ass. In other moments, I was chubby, or tired, or clever, or a fraidy cat, or a right fielder.

"He's half Jewish, half asleep," my mother assessed.

Are we ever who we think we are? How is that possible, if our thoughts are constantly changing?

I thought I was an honor student, then that bastard gave me a C+ in Social Studies.

Until we understand monkey mind, we identify with the monkeys, swinging from thought to thought, story to story.

THE MONKEYS

I wake in the night to a strange, intense burning in my chest. "Great," I think, "I'm having a heart attack."

This is what the Jungle Doctor calls a colored thought. The uncolored thought would simply be:

"I feel a burning in my chest."

But then I colored it with a story. Heart disease in my family. My father dead at 64, his father at 53...

I drink some water and the burning goes away. It was heartburn.

We look at others and think, "What are they *thinking*?" But how often do we notice our own thoughts?

We average between 12,000 and 60,000 thoughts a day. Where do they all come from?

The Jungle Doctor identifies five sources.

"He knows all the Presidents," my mother tells company.

"Let's hear!" someone says.

I stand up and recite them in order, all 37, from George Washington to Richard M. Nixon, and then bow to the applause.

The first source of thoughts is right knowledge. These are the thoughts that make us think we're smart. Or even powerful. That's why they say knowledge is power.

Right knowledge comes from:

1. *Direct experience*. We know there's a fire, because we're roasting our marshmallows in it.

2. *Sound reasoning.* We see smoke, and where there's smoke, there's fire.

3. *A reliable source.* The Fire Marshall says there's a fire.

It's good to know where we get our knowledge. And if it's worth knowing in the first place.

I get in the elevator and there's Chris. As always, he's impecabbly dressed. And never a hair out of place, which is why I like to muss it.

Except this time, he's horrified. As if I never mussed it before.

Turns out, it's not Chris. It's Jason, his identical twin, who's been interviewing for a job with the company.

The second source of thoughts is wrong knowledge.

Wrong knowledge is based soley on appearance.

The newsletter goes out on April Fool's Day. I figure it'll be funny to make up a story.

Turns out, it's not so funny. One response in appreciation of the dark humor. Three unsubscribes. One person that we know of is deeply disturbed by it.

The third source of thoughts is fiction—words with no basis in reality.

Even when you know something's not real, imagination goes to work, leaving an impression in the mind. I say *a rabbit with horns* and there it is, however you picture it.

The Koreans have a proverb:

Words have no wings but they can fly a thousand miles.

The loss is hard to bear. I sleep late, nap all afternoon, and go to bed after supper. It seems to work—until I wake up and there it is, the loss, right there waiting for me.

The fourth source of thoughts—including the thought that we can just disappear—is deep, dreamless sleep.

Every night, during that phase in our sleep cycle, it's like our minds keep taking pictures with the lens cap on, deepening our impression of nothingness.

If we identify with that impression, we think we can erase ourselves and our thoughts. All we have to do is go back to sleep, get drunk, gamble, go shopping, or however we choose to go dark.

Nacky would take me along when he checked his muskrat traps. Sometimes he'd catch one or two, but most of the traps would be empty, or sprung, needing to be reset.

This is memory, the fifth source of thoughts.

Our minds are like those traps, clenching to objects or experiences from our past.

THE FOUR DELUSIONS

He points to various places on the X-ray. "See these? You're getting long in the tooth."

Long in the tooth? What the hell does that mean?

It means bone loss. He wants to make a mold of my mouth, then send me to "his guy," an orthodonist who will remove some of the teeth and insert implants to anchor a bridge.

What? How can this be? I've had perfect teeth my entire life! Just one cavity!

The problem, you see, isn't my teeth. It's my mind.

This is the first delusion:

Seeing the impermanent as permanent.

Walking the dog, I see the political sign in their front yard. How could anyone in their right mind vote for that bozo?

You know what? I can let it go. The man's on the porch, reading the paper. I'll wave, maybe even say hello.

This is the second delusion: seeing the impure as pure.

My intent to wave isn't pure. It has nothing to do with being neighborly. It's to prove to myself how spiritual I am to forgive him for being an idiot.

I slow down, waiting for him to look up, but he keeps reading.

Jimmy and Rosemary give me a case of a limited-release beer, brewed in small batches each summer.

It's made with honey and natural lemonade flavor. The first few sips are cool and refreshing. The alcohol buzz is pleasing.

But then it gets warmer, and doesn't taste as good. I don't have the tolerance for more than two bottles. The buzz is already fading.

This is the third delusion: Seeing dissatisfaction as happiness.

It started when Anita Goldberg lost her husband.

"You're such a good writer," said my mother. "Can't you write her a nice note?"

So I sat down and wrote. I wrote about Arthur's passion for televised golf, how he'd forget about the cigar in his mouth and have to keep relighting it. It was a lovely letter. Anita kept it in her purse and showed it to everyone.

Long story short, I'm a writer. writer12345@yahoo.com is my email address.

This is the fourth delusion: seeing the nonessential self as essential.

Who would I be if I stopped writing?

Carson McCullers once wrote a story about a writer who couldn't write.

"How could you dare to write such a story?" said Tennessee Williams. "It's the most terrifying work I ever read."

THE FOUR ATTACHMENTS

"His heart's in the right place, and he's doing the best he can, but he doesn't know what he's doing. No judgment, just saying."

When I talk like this, I think I'm being objective.

This is self-centeredness, caused by the attachment to thinking. It's when you identify with the thinker, and end up like the statue by Rodin, lost in thought.

While there might be some truth to what I'm saying about the guy, it doesn't feel good, because I've separated myself from him by conceptualizing him. I'm not really *seeing* him, or myself for that matter.

The more we identify with the thinker, the more isolated we become.

Don't play too much chess.

For the millionth time, I turn Lily upside down and sing the silly little song.

"Again!" she says.

This is attachment to pleasure, caused by the craving to repeat the feeling.

Twelve years later, when I drop her off at college, I'm the one who's attached.

If this plane lands safely, the pilot might want to think twice about coming out to thank us as we deboard, because I may just punch his face in. There's been turbulence since we took off three hours ago and he hasn't said a word about it.

This is aversion, attachment to an unpleasant experience from the past and not wanting to repeat it.

Back when Delta's slogan was *We love to fly and it shows*, I also loved to fly—until a rocky, low-altitude flight with no announcements freaked me out.

Now I sing: *I hate to fly 'cause it blows*.

My mother says you can get used to hanging if you do it long enough.

Who would we be without our suffering, without all of our habits and views that make us and everyone else miserable?

Some would call it an identity crisis.

The Jungle Doctor calls it fear of death—the death of who we think we are.

This is the final attachment: attaching to all the other attachments.

THE ANTIDOTE

REQUIREMENTS FOR SEATED MEDITATION

- a simple chair or cushion
- patience

1. ALIGN YOUR BODY FOR STABILITY AND COMFORT

The body is first. Until you can sit still, seated meditation is almost impossible. If you have physical issues, modify these instructions as necessary.

Foundation: If using a cushion, knees should be level with or below the hips, ideally on the ground. If this isn't happening, use a chair. The chair should be simple and firm, not too cushy. If possible, sit forward so you're not leaning against the back of the chair. Feet are flat on the ground under the knees.

Spine: Whether on a cushion or chair, root your sitting bones and lift your ribs enough to decompress the lower back and take any pressure off your tailbone. Lift your breastbone slightly, feeling a sense of dignity and alertness. Relax your shoulders. Chin is parallel to the floor and slightly in toward your throat until you feel your neck lengthen.

Hands: Rest them on your thighs or lap so they're supported and relaxed, close enough to the torso so there's no pulling or effort to keep them there. Hands and arms are dead weight. No need for mudras (hand gestures). Keep it simple.

Eyes: Keep them open, resting your gaze softly on a blank wall in front of you or on the floor a few feet ahead. If this makes you dizzy or nauseous, close your eyes.

If you're seated on a cushion and need to recross your legs, do so meditatively and immediately return to stillness. Practice aligning your body until you can sit comfortably without moving. Then proceed to Step 2.

2. RELAX DEEPLY WHILE STAYING ALIGNED

Relax all muscles, major and minor, that you don't need to maintain your alignment. Meet any tension you notice with conscious relaxation.

Feel how deeply your body can relax. Breathe naturally. You can use your exhalations to keep letting go.

Relax into stillness and be aware of that stillness. Keep practicing this step until you can sit comfortably still for 10 minutes.

If your body doesn't feel stable or comfortable, return to Step 1.

3. FEEL YOUR BREATH

Don't manipulate your breath. Let it be natural, and simply rest your attention on how it feels. Feel it directly, in one place where the sensations are most noticeable: either the nostrils or the abdomen. Rest your attention on the sensations of breathing. If you notice the mind wandering, gently come back to feeling the breath.

Practice this for at least 20 minutes, until your attention rests easily and naturally on your breath. If your body becomes prohibitively uncomfortable, cycle back through Steps 1 & 2 and then continue practicing this step.

4. ALLOW YOUR BREATH TO QUIET

Never suppress your breath; let it quiet naturally. Then rest attention on the quiet breath. Notice the urge to think or shift attention. Keep quietude at the forefront, even as thoughts, feelings or sounds arise.

Cycle back through previous steps as necessary until you can sit easily for 30 minutes, with moments of the mind at rest, aware but not thinking.

Sit longer as desired, but sit at least once a day every day.

If 30 minutes is too long, start with five or ten. The quality of your attention and effort is more important than the duration. Better to sit two minutes with awareness than an hour without it.

FREQUENTLY ASKED QUESTIONS

Do I really have to meditate every day?

The practice is established with regularity. Otherwise you won't get the full benefits or you might quit. Make it a no-brainer, like brushing your teeth. Make sure to bring some enthusiasm and curiosity to your practice. You shouldn't feel like you're torturing yourself.

I have arthritis in my hips and it's painful to sit. Can I lie down instead?

It's better to sit up if you can find a way. If you lie down, it's easy to space out or fall asleep. Experiment with ways to sit up, and if you end up on your back, remain vigilant.

Is it better to sit on a cushion than in a chair?

No, it just depends on your body. Try both and see which affords you the most stability and comfort.

Why eyes open instead of closed?

Eyes open helps keep you present. It's easier to space out with the eyes closed.

I have an extremely active monkey mind. Is there something additional I can do to quiet it down?

Just be aware. Notice the thoughts and let them pass like clouds in the sky. Be the sky. This isn't about getting rid of thoughts; it's about changing your relationship to them.

What about music? Or guided meditations or visualizations?

It's best not to introduce additional content. Be attentive to the content that's already there—bodily sensations, breath, thoughts. Keep it simple.

I have respiratory issues. Sometimes I have a hard time breathing.

Just breathe as you need to. If it's too disturbing to rest attention on the breath, feel bodily sensations instead. Just get as relaxed and as attentive as you can.

I have a lot of anxiety, and sometimes sitting makes it worse.

Then don't sit. Anything can be a meditation: walking, swimming, doing a puzzle—any solitary activity that you enjoy. The main thing is to be relaxed and attentive to what you're doing.

I've been getting into this deep, dreamy state between sleeping and waking. It's very pleasant, but I'm wondering if that's good.

As long as you stay aware. Try not to space out. If you feel drowsy, widen your eyes, check your posture, whatever you have to do. Depth is good, but keep paying attention.

What about coffee?

If it keeps you from nodding off, drink it.

Nothing seems to be happening for me. How long should I give it?

Sometimes the changes are gradual, and not easy to notice. Give it 40 days, and don't attach to any results or outcomes. Expectations only get in the way.

Can you recommend other books on meditation?

You yourself are a billion-page book packed with wisdom. Read you. Stick to the practice, and the books you're asking about will come along.

APPENDIX

THE FIVE SOURCES OF THOUGHT

- Right knowledge
- Wrong knowledge
- Fiction
- Deep sleep
- Memory

THE FOUR DELUSIONS

- Seeing the impermanent as permanent
- Seeing impure intent as pure
- Seeing dissatisfaction as happiness
- Seeing the unessential as the essential self

THE FOUR ATTACHMENTS

- Attachment To Thinking
- Attachment To Craving
- Attachment To Avoiding
- Attachment To Suffering

SEATED MEDITATION

- Align the body for stability and comfort
- Relax into stillness while maintaining alignment
- Feel the natural breath
- Allow the breath to quiet

ACKNOWLEDGMENTS

I'd like to thank Khamkéo Vilaysing, Hari Jap and Connor, Ruth Price, The World Book Encyclopedia, Mr. Dean, Chris and Jason McKee, Steve Nack, Dr. Weissman, our neighbor at 24th Street & Cinnabar, Jimmy and Rosemary Gifford, Jacob Leinenkugel Brewing Company, Anita Goldberg, Carson McCullers, Tennessee Williams, Lily Price, and Delta Airlines.

ALSO BY STEVE PRICE

Crab Apples: Stories & Poems
Song of Scott
Brake Light
They Don't Have A Word For It
Narcissus: The Man, The Myth, The Flower
John Doe's Diamond
Arrows of Love: A New Version of The Bhagavad Gita
A Bowler's View of the Tao Te Ching
Crawling Back To Patanjali
Assembly Instructions for Your Head
Writing From Scratch
How's Your Ice Cream?
Swami On Call
Coping With Bliss
Song of the Heart With No Walls
Clam In The Sky
Rocky (with Olive Price)
Can I Have One Moment of Peace?
Journal of Lovesickness, Vol. 11

To learn more, visit onemomentofpeace.org.

www.ingramcontent.com/pod-product-compliance
Lightning Source LLC
Chambersburg PA
CBHW051406150726
48000CB00003B/1358